Reading Program Book 8: homophones

Clifford's Field Day

by Donna Taylor

Illustrated by Josie Yee

Based on the books by Norman Bridwell

SCHOLASTIC INC.
New York Toronto London Auckland Sydney
Mexico City New Delhi Hong Kong Buenos Aires

It was Field Day at Emily Elizabeth's school. It was a great day with a bright sun and a blue sky. All kinds of sports events were taking place. Everyone was happy and excited. The three-legged race was about to begin. Miss Carrington blew her whistle.

Emily Elizabeth and Charley started to run along together. But Clifford wanted to race, too.

"No, Clifford," said Emily Elizabeth. "You know you can't do that! Go, sit! Please!"

Then came the sack race. Emily Elizabeth really wanted to win this one. But Clifford ran away with her sack — while Emily Elizabeth was still inside it! He thought he was helping her win. But Jetta was the one who won the race.

Next came time to jump the horse. When it was Emily Elizabeth's turn, Clifford got onto the springboard.

Emily Elizabeth looked Clifford in the eye. "I want to jump," she said. "Please let me do it alone. Okay, Clifford?"

Clifford got off the springboard. He let Emily Elizabeth jump alone. Then…he jumped. He jumped higher than anyone did.

At the kickball game, Charley rolled the ball to Emily Elizabeth. Emily Elizabeth kicked the ball. But Clifford ran around the bases!

Clifford hit the ball at the softball game and he won the relay race — by himself! No one could beat him.

Emily Elizabeth's face was red as a beet. Charley started laughing. Then Jetta and Vaz laughed. Miss Carrington laughed.

And finally Emily Elizabeth did, too.

"The whole day belongs to Clifford," said Miss Carrington. "I never knew he was so good at sports. He beat us at everything!"

"He sure did," said Emily Elizabeth. "I'm proud of him. He is…

...the new champ!"